Love on the Rocks

Louisa Loder

Compiled and published by Serenity Press

Copyright © 2016 Serenity Press

All rights reserved. No part of this book may be used or reproduced by any means, graphic, electronic, or mechanical, including photocopying, recording, taping or by any information storage retrieval system without the written permission of the copyright owner except in the case of brief quotations embodied in critical articles and reviews.

Serenity Press books may be ordered through online booksellers or by contacting:
www.serenitypress.org
publisher@serenitypress.org
editor@serenitypress.org

Because of the dynamic nature of the Internet, any web addresses or links contained in this book may have changed since publication and may no longer be valid. The views expressed in this work are solely those of the authors and do not necessarily reflect the views of the publisher and the publisher hereby disclaims any responsibility for them.

The author(s) of this book do not dispense medical advice or prescribe the use of any technique as a form of treatment for physical, emotional, or medical problems without the advice of a physician, either directly or indirectly. The intent of the author(s) is only to offer information of a general nature to help you. In the event you use any of the information in this book for yourself, which is your constitutional right, the author(s) and the publisher assume no responsibility for your actions.

ISBN: 978-0-9953976-8-2

Love on the Rocks

His hands were everywhere, even places where Kate hadn't known she'd needed to be touched. At first she had responded greedily, her fingers running over his well-muscled shoulders before dipping down the curve of his biceps. She had been set to blaze a trail down to the uncharted territory of his chest when his hand captured hers and held them tightly in place. The molten heat of his breath against her ear had done enough to urge her forward, while also warning her to stay perfectly still.

Somewhere in the receding part of her mind that was still capable of rational thought, Kate admitted that the evening had been a success.

It hadn't started out that way.

Kate's first hurdle had been deciding what to wear. She'd never experienced this kind of indecision about fashion before. Dressing up or down, or anywhere in between had earned her something of a reputation in her circle of friends for always being 'on trend', if a little conservative. But the bouquet of cute-dress-and-cardigan combos in her wardrobe were far from *enticing*, and just throwing on jeans and a sexy top felt like cheating, somehow. Luckily, her go-to opinion buzzed through on her phone just in the nick of time.

'Hey, Luce,' Kate smiled, cradling her mobile between her cheek and shoulder as she flicked through clothes hangers.

'What're you up to?' Luce was the kind of friend who was wonderfully spontaneous. 'I thought we could head to Dome and get some cake. Screw the diet,' she added, sounding typically avante garde, 'I need something sweet.'

'That'd be nice,' replied Kate diplomatically, 'but I'm going speed-dating tonight.'

There was a long silence from the other end of the line.

'Please tell me you're kidding.'

'I'm kidding.' Kate lied on auto-pilot, but couldn't smooth the amusement out of her voice.

'What about Greg?' Luce asked pointedly.

Kate hesitated. 'What *about* Greg?' she shot back, looking through her large selection of tops. Things between them hadn't been wonderful of late. The intimacy had been rushed at best, and non-existent at worst. 'Maybe we both need to see what we're missing out on.'

Luce sighed noisily on the other end of the phone. 'Oh, Kate. What's going on?'

Love on the Rocks

'Nothing,' said Kate defensively. Then, under her breath, 'but hopefully not for much longer.'

'Where is he?'

Where, indeed. 'Working this weekend,' Kate lied. Instantly, her stomach churned. She'd never had to keep the truth from Luce before. But she couldn't tell her everything about Greg. The secret needed to be theirs, just for now.

Tell-tale sounds let Kate know her recently non-smoking bestie had just lit up. Luce always smoked when things made her feel anxious. During her two marriage breakups, Luce had practically been on fire.

'It's your divorce,' Luce said flippantly. 'But speed dating, Kate? Really?' Luce whined in a way that made it plain that while she didn't approve, she would support her friend anyway. 'It's *so* 2005.'

By this time, Kate's smile felt distinctly more genuine. She plucked out a denim pencil skirt and tossed it onto the bed as a possibility. 'Really. Well, at least as soon as I can figure out what to wear.'

'As little as possible, if you're going to go through with it,' Luce advised immediately. 'You'll need every advantage, if you've got to wow someone in five minutes.'

'Not helpful,' Kate laughed. 'And it's six minutes.'

'Specific,' Luce said. 'I like it. Where's this delightful mating ritual taking place?'

'The Pig.'

Another long silence. Kate knew Luce's thoughts on the local pub, and had taken deliberate relish in stirring her friend up.

'Good luck,' came the sage words drifting from Kate's mobile, 'and Godspeed.'

The second hurdle had arrived in the form of instant mortification. Arriving at the well-known local pub, Kate realised that she was by far the oldest woman there — everyone else looked like they were in their early twenties. Again, her usual buffers weren't there to fall back on. The girls would have laughed it off with her, and they could have spent the night having a good time. She pushed her shoulders back, owning the compromise she had finally worn with a confidence she was far from feeling. A denim pencil skirt and a sheer white blouse could be sexy, if she wanted them to be. The cardigan draped over her arm was for backup. She had no idea what sort of people she'd meet at an event like this.

Then again, even being there in the first place was a coup for her. Being married to Greg for five years had lulled her into a false sense of security. It had been easy to look to him for reassurance on issues affecting their lives, without knowing the damage that was doing to *her* life. As a bank manager, he had strict ideals on what life should be and how it should roll out. Having their daughter, Jenna, had proven to him that not everything went according to plan. It just went to show you that life definitely threw a wicked curve-ball once in a while.

Kate's smile was firmly in place as she checked her watch. She was early.

Love on the Rocks

'I'll have an orange juice please,' she said to the barmaid. She had a feeling she would need to keep her wits about her, even though it was tempting to try to drown her nerves in vodka. There would be plenty of time for real drinks later; hopefully with a side of tall, handsome, and adventurous. The warmth of the room's wood panelling comforted Kate as she sipped her juice, and waited for the other speed-daters arrive.

It was early enough that there were only a few other people in the room. A group of ladies were clustered around a table across the room, their conversation interrupted by loud bursts of raucous laughter. A man sat on a stool further down the bar, his hand curled around a glass of what looked like straight whiskey, making Kate raise an eyebrow with interest. There wasn't much about the Swinging Pig to indicate that it was for the single-malt types, but then she supposed that it didn't have a reputation for catering to juice-swiggers either. She began to dig about in her bag for her phone, her go-to defence mechanism when sitting alone.

'Single?'

Kate glanced up. The man with the whiskey was looking her way, but he spoke with such an assumed familiarity that she turned to see if he was talking to someone behind her. He was undeniably attractive, with dark blonde hair that had been artfully messed into a style she'd always told Greg would look good on him, if he'd ever dared to try something different. His eyes were an arresting shade of oceanic grey. They reminded Kate of cold, deep water. For a moment, she felt as though she'd have to take a breath, in case she got in over her head. And then he smirked at her, in a way that told her that he was a man completely used to getting his own way.

Instantly, she was determined that he would be disappointed.

A frown flickered across her features, as she blinked. Had he really just tried to find out whether she was available in the space of two syllables? A look of disbelief finally settled on her face.

'I beg your pardon?

If he noticed that she was taken aback, he didn't let it show. In fact, he seemed amused by her reaction to his directness. His smirk was skewed, hovering on one side of his lips as he made a show of glancing around the almost empty room. 'You don't look like you're meeting anyone,' he explained, lifting his glass for a swig.

Kate glared at him for a second, wondering whether it would be worth giving him a dressing down. 'I'm meeting people, actually,' she told him loftily. 'You might find it an interesting concept, but there's more to most people than their relationship status.'

'Oh.' He took a sip of his whiskey. He savoured the taste, before he downed it. His eyes never left hers, though the smug look on his face had simmered down. 'I just thought you might have been here for the speed dating,' he said casually.

Love on the Rocks

Oh shit. Kate's stomach did a somersault. Was *he* here for the speed dating? He didn't look it. His jeans were business-casual neat, his smart polo peeking from beneath his artfully distressed leather jacket. Her interest in him swerved hard to the right, to avoid the pothole he had left in the road by interrupting her so rudely in the first place. She realised that her gaze had fallen to rest on the tempting way he filled out the jacket, and quickly looked away from his arms. In an attempt to save her dignity, Kate lifted her chin. Her chestnut curls bobbed with the action as she looked him square in the eyes. 'I am.'

The lopsided smirk that mocked her earlier broke through the cloud cover of his otherwise serious expression. He dipped his head slightly, as though trying to peer more directly into her eyes. 'Then you *are* single?'

She shouldn't have gotten goose bumps as a result of that smarmy line. She shouldn't have felt flummoxed, as though she didn't have a comeback waiting to wipe the smug look from his (chiselled, intense) face. But words failed her. Kate turned back to her juice, embarrassed, annoyed, and more than a little bit intrigued. The last sensation only served to make her *more* annoyed.

'Sorry,' she began, in a tone that betrayed the fact she wasn't sorry in the slightest, 'but that's a really weird question to introduce yourself to someone with.'

He swivelled on his stool to face her properly. His arm leaned casually on the bar, his hand still curled protectively around his whiskey glass. 'But I haven't introduced myself,' he said, the smirk fading.

The hostess of the evening chose that moment to make her grand entrance. Her ridiculously coiffed fake blonde wig and Marilyn-esque dress went a long way towards making Kate feel less ridiculous herself. She swanned across the floor in a flurry of white chiffon and a feather boa, smiling widely at the people who had started to arrive during the strange, tense conversation at the bar. Both Kate and the mysterious Single Malt turned to look at her, but as soon as Marilyn passed, Kate's attention came full circle. She plucked her bag from its perch on the stool between them, and hopped off her own in what she hoped was an appropriately sassy manner.

'And you needn't bother to,' Kate snapped, before following in Marilyn's peep-toed footsteps.

The other people gathered in the smaller area off the main bar were dressed more like Kate, which meant that she could smile with them at their hostess' outlandish appearance. After setting up her 'wares' on a nearby bar table, she gestured to the gathered hopefuls to come closer and listen up. Kate shuffled closer, near a younger looking man with loads of gel in his hair, as far away from the rude stranger as she could manage.

'Hi there,' the hostess breathed, in a clear attempt to sound like her celebrity muse. 'Everyone's gonna need to put on one of these little wrist bands,' she held up a bunch of purple paper strips, 'and grab a scorecard.' Marilyn executed a graceful gesture. Kate wondered how long it had taken to perfect the manoeuvre. A small, supposedly coy

Love on the Rocks

smile lingered on Marilyn's bright red lips. 'Ladies, take a seat and the boys'll come to you. You'll have six minutes with each fella, and then we'll switch things up. At the end of the round, you'll get your free drink from the bar and can mingle to your heart's content. Any questions?'

'I'm not used to only having six minutes to get down to business,' Hair Gel said jokingly.

There was a slight bubble of laughter from the group, before the women moved to sit down. The only person who didn't smile was the man from the bar, who rolled his eyes and almost seemed bored with the whole affair. He glanced Kate's way and caught her looking at him, her laughter at the joke still plain on her face. Lifting her eyebrows and shrugging a shoulder at him, Kate was still smiling as she made her way through the crowd towards an empty stool.

'So I'll have paid off the house before I hit forty, and be ready to take my dream holiday to Monaco.'

'Great.' Kate regurgitated the word. It was apt, because it was exactly what Tom Lane (thirty-six, real estate agent, golfer, non-smoker) thought he was. Four minutes in and counting, she realised meeting him wasn't a total loss. He'd already given her some *great* tips about where to 'invest strategically'. Before long, though, her attention had wandered. He was too much like Greg, who always had an evolving five-year plan. Plans so often went awry that Kate had learned to think of them for what they were: restrictions.

'The best thing about what I do,' Tom continued with a smile that made him look more politician than playboy, 'is that it leaves plenty of time to hit the gym.' His eyes travelled over Kate's exposed upper arms appraisingly. 'D'you like to work out, Kate?'

Even as she started to answer, Kate reached for her trusty cardigan. She put it on, and then looked back to Tom, but her gaze was distracted by the man from the bar. He was leaning back on his stool, arms crossed over his chest, as he chatted to a seemingly bubbly blonde woman. He looked bored out his head, but his date hadn't seemed to notice. 'Not really,' Kate said slowly, re-focusing on Tom with a smile that was stretched forcefully across her face. 'I don't really have the time or energy after I run around for my daughter.'

Tom seemed taken aback, as Kate shrugged into her lavender-knit armour. 'Oh,' Tom replied awkwardly, glancing down at the cheap plastic alarm clock that was sitting on the table between them. It was ticking down like a bomb they had failed to defuse in time. 'You have a daughter? How old?'

'Eleven,' she said brightly.

'Ah,' he said. To his credit, he at least *tried* to sound interested. 'What school does she go to?'

To *her* credit, Kate really could have cared less. 'Rocky Beach.'

The buzzer chirped and Kate thought she could see visible relief on Tom's perfectly moisturised face. She was sure his ideal holiday to saucy Monaco and the thought of paying off his house had been threatened by visions of a bratty eleven year old with braces demanding his precious time and money. Shuffling a little on the hard wooden stool, Kate wondered whether Jenna would have as huge an impact on *all* men the way she had seemed to have on Tom Lane.

Tom stood, offering her an efficient nod-smile better suited to a trendy Freo night spot where it was too noisy to effect a real farewell. Although she hated to admit it, Kate felt cagey about not being able to see the rude man from before. He lingered somewhere in the space behind her now, having moved on from his first date. She had an acute awareness of his presence, as though he was glancing at her behind her back.

Ignoring the feeling, she took a breath and reached to pour herself a glass of water.

If it had been difficult to get a word in edgewise with Tom, Kate found entirely the opposite was the case with Anthony James (thirty-eight, counsellor, mountain biker, Dockers supporter, extreme user of hair gel).

'What do you do, Kate? Oh, event management — did you need to go to uni for that? Where do you live? What do you enjoy doing in your spare time? Do you have any brothers or sisters? Have you travelled? What is your idea of a perfect date? What kind of movies …'

She answered all questions in good faith, if not with feigned enthusiasm for the topic. Any attempt by her to steer the conversation back to *his* hobbies, or *his* favourite anything was met with quick self-deprecation, which might have been charming if it hadn't seemed utterly fake. It wasn't until Anthony asked her whether she enjoyed growing up with a large family that she realised he hadn't been listening to a single word she'd said.

'I already told you that I only have one brother,' Kate said trying to hide her annoyance. 'Hardly a big family, but I suppose I enjoyed having him around. It's harder now, with him living in Sydney.'

'Yeah, I can imagine it is,' Anthony said, missing the warning signs. 'But at least—'

The way he bungled on made Kate furious. She held up a hand, not wanting to be rude but determined to pull the plug on what was rapidly becoming an awkward situation. 'Sorry,' she began, stopping Anthony from whatever sensitive-man mumbo jumbo he'd been likely to spout. 'But is this really working for you?'

Anthony blinked, mouth agape. This kind of response obviously hadn't been part of his rehearsal process. 'The date?'

'The routine,' Kate said, trying to be kind despite her irritation. 'You're so intent on being a good listener than you're not *actually* listening.'

The poor man flushed at having been caught out, and looked for a second as though he might bluster at her and attempt a cover up. He thought better of it, and instead adopted a more natural stance, his shoulders losing their rigid poise. A long sigh escaped him.

Love on the Rocks

'Sorry,' he said sheepishly, allowing himself a shake of his head. 'It's just ... it's been a while since I did this. I've just split up from my wife — well, not 'just' — it was six months ago. But I suppose I'm still adjusting.'

Kate instantly felt sorry for him. She could relate to feeling nervous, after having been with one person for such a long time. Reaching out across the table, she placed her hand over Anthony's. He looked at her curiously. 'Don't worry about it,' she told him. 'It was nice to meet you, either way. And hey – the next date is the next date. But if you're going to ask her a question, *really* listen. And give her the chance to listen to you, too.'

There it was again – that strange feeling of being watched.

Kate reclaimed her hand, and sat back.

Anthony glanced down at her sticky-label name tag, betraying the fact that he hadn't even listened when she'd introduced herself. 'Thanks Kate,' he said with a genuine smile.

'These blokes are definitely not my type,' Kate muttered into the phone as she bent towards the mirror in the ladies' toilet. She had her lippy in one hand, and Luce's wisdom in the other.

'Of course not,' Luce laughed as Kate pressed her lips together. 'You married a banker, for God's sake. I can't believe you actually went.'

Kate sighed, popping her war paint back into her bag. 'Do you think I should just go home?'

'Is there *anyone* there that might make it worth the trouble of agonising over which nanna cardigan you were going to wear?' Luce asked, bluntly.

Kate's mind instantly landed on the one man she didn't want to count, with a flashback to his intense eyes, and then his tantalising smirk. 'They're not nanna cardigans,' she argued in a low voice, stubbornly pushing him out of her thoughts.

'Whatever,' Luce said. 'I'm not saying you need to update your wardrobe or anything. Just that it might be better if you started shopping at Adult Temptations instead of … where *do* you get those bloody cardigans from?'

Kate left the bathroom, her phone still pressed to her ear, and began to make her way back to the Speed Dating Bonanza when voices drifting from the slightly open door of the men's bathroom caught her attention.

Wasn't there a saying that eavesdroppers never heard anything good about themselves? Against her better judgement, Kate hovered.

'Total MILF,' was the first comment she heard properly. Surprise registered on her face, her eyes widening and mouth dropping open. She thought she recognised the voice.

'What?' Kate *definitely* recognised the second voice. It was the man from the bar — Mr Cool. She stood in the corridor, phone pressed between ear and shoulder, and pretended to be looking for something in her bag. Her ears strained to pick up the thread of conversation among the din of the pub. It was getting busier.

'The chick I talked to first. Katie, I think her name was.' Tom Lane. *Unbelievable*. She'd known he wasn't the kind of guy she was interested in seeing. It was sickening and relieving to have her thoughts confirmed so thoroughly.

There was a short silence. 'Are you joking?' Mr Cool's short, clipped tones implied he wasn't amused.

'No way!' laughed Tom. 'She'd be stunning in a little bikini, up on the Sunshine Coast somewhere. Shame about the kid.'

If her mouth opened any further, Kate would be in real danger of saying something she would regret. Curiosity drove her further down the corridor. She craned her neck, desperately trying to see through the gap in the doorway. As luck would have it, she could see a sliver of Tom's back and part of Mr Cool's face in the grimy mirror on the wall.

'Kate?' Luce asked impatiently.

'Watch your mouth,' Mr Cool snapped. It looked like he was ready to lose it.

'Huh?' Tom sounded surprised. 'What the hell are you on about, mate? You haven't even spoken to the bird yet.'

'I don't need to. And she's not a bird. Show some respect.' Mr Cool's face had the same intense glare Kate had glimpsed at the bar. She blinked quickly, not wanting to miss the show.

'Hey man,' Tom chuckled, 'don't stress — it's all good! I'm not going there. If she's already pulled a swift one on some poor dude keeping her in child support, I'm not about to line up for seconds.'

There was a sudden clang. Kate jumped and gasped with surprise. She saw Tom's reflection stumble back into the mirror, his hand shooting out to grab the metal hand dryer on the wall. A moment later, Mr Cool stepped into full view. Tom scrambled to stand up straight, tugging down the front of his shirt where it seemed to have been pulled.

'What the hell!' he shouted.

'Kate?' Luce's voice in her ear was concerned. 'Hello? Are you okay? Is there a brawl happening? Do you need me to call for back-up?'

'Shh!' Kate hissed, straining to hear. Mr Cool was saying something, his voice low and dangerous, but before she could make it out, the door to the men's bathroom was wrenched open. Kate scrambled across the corridor to slip into the ladies' toilet before anyone noticed her skulking about, but in her effort to make it as far into the feminine sanctuary as possible, she nearly bowled into another lady leaving the bathroom. 'Oh, sorry,' she spluttered, shuffling to one side to get out of the way. The woman had light coloured hair, more silver than blonde, and pinned Kate with a stern, unimpressed look. Kate barely had time to notice their matching lavender cardigans before the woman made her stately way through the door.

Love on the Rocks

If she hadn't been surprised to actually *see* a nanna wearing her cardigan, Kate would have asked the woman if the coast was clear.

The bathroom was suddenly quiet all around her, save for the residual music she could hear vibrating through the tiled walls. Kate took a moment to collect herself, and then remembered her phone.

'Luce?' she said slowly, her eyes still pinned to the door as though she expected Mr Cool to invade the ladies' loo.

'Finally.' Luce sounded relieved. 'I thought you were dead.'

'Not yet,' Kate said, 'but I *am* going to have to call you later.'

By the time Marcus Shadwell (thirty-five, brickie, great smile, dog lover) came over to her small table, Kate no longer felt her backside. The small stool she perched on did her no favours in the comfort department, and Kate stood to greet Marcus so she could stretch her legs. He shook her hand, and Kate noticed how warm and weathered his hand was. He wore a surf shirt and jeans with casual charm, and his tousled brown hair led Kate to think that Marcus could be a contender. Her heartbeat quickened as he smiled at her. She tried not to be distracted by his easy manners and the wholesome warmth in his velvety brown eyes.

But Kate's senses seemed to have other plans for her attention. She was acutely aware that the man from the bar now sat with the girl next to her. Kate heard snippets of their conversation, and fought the urge to turn her head for a proper look at the woman who laughed softly at the next table over. Instead, she focused her attention on Marcus who, it turned out, loved to go bushwalking with his dog.

'Great Danes are gorgeous dogs,' she smiled, leaning toward him with interest.

'She's a dream,' he grinned. 'People have the most amazing reaction to her. Animals are awesome. They just have this calming effect on people, don't you think?'

Kate grinned back. He had a kind of light about him that was infectious, and Kate didn't mind getting caught up in it. 'She's lucky to have someone to love her like you do,' she said.

Marcus met her gaze, his wide smile firmly in place. 'I've always loved animals. You're welcome to come and meet her any time you like,' he offered.

Kate smiled as her stomach somersaulted. What would life be like with a guy like Marcus? He seemed to enjoy taking life one moment at a time; it might be nice to actually appreciate time for what it was — a series of special, connected moments. Greg always had things scheduled down to the last moment, determined to squeeze as much as possible into every day. Kate found herself smiling as she thought of how much her husband would hate to let things in life happen naturally, rather than influencing them.

'Maybe I will,' she promised, as the buzzer chirped the end of their time.

Love on the Rocks

When she heard movement at the table next to her, Kate glanced over quickly to see Mr Cool getting up to move on to his next table. *Her* table.

She made sure she was positioned comfortably by the time he sat down. Her eyes were fixed on the rapidly melting ice cubes in her juice when she heard him put down his drink. She smoothed down her already-smooth skirt. Finally, Kate glanced up, when she could think of no other excuse *not* to.

He wasn't wearing his name tag, which instantly made Kate regret having kept hers on. When he looked at her calmly, one leather-covered arm leaning arrogantly on the table, the scent of his cologne wafted tantalisingly around her. It tempted her with its woody, masculine aroma. Kate's mind leapt into a wishful flash-forward, and for a moment she thought about how he would smell up close and personal. She fought back a blush, pushing the unhelpful image away.

He was amused; there was a small crinkling just around the corners of his eyes that would have made him look approachable, if he wasn't likely to speak and ruin the effect.

'I think we're probably going to have to go through with that introduction now,' he managed with a smirk.

Kate sat up straighter, her chin lifting defiantly. 'Rules were meant to be broken.'

Her smile was smug, but it wasn't able to stand up to the way he looked back at her. His head fell back slightly, making him look even cockier and more self-assured. His eyes were bleak; the heat they previously hinted at had been washed away. He reminded her of a modern-day Mr. Darcy — aloof, with one heck of a superiority complex. Surely at least four minutes under his withering glare had passed already?

She squirmed inwardly, feeling a stirring in her emotions that was part irritation, part lust. It made her feel uncomfortable, as though she was betraying herself while admitting her attraction to him. Determined to regain her self-control, if not her attitude, she forced up an eyebrow.

'Kate.'

'Roman,' he replied, shifting slightly on his stool before folding his arms.

'You're kidding,' she scoffed, glad his name was ridiculous enough to distract her from the way his jacket clung in all the right places.

Roman's eyebrows shot up, before pulling together in a frown. 'No,' he said crisply. 'I'm *not*.'

Kate finally felt as though she had the upper hand. No matter how sexy his moody eyes were when they fixed themselves on her, there was no way she would be bested by a guy called *Roman*.

'I'd say it's a pleasure to meet you,' she smiled sweetly, 'but I'm a terrible liar.'

He reached out to grab his glass. 'You might be wrong,' he warned her.

She looked at him dubiously. 'About?'

That roguish gleam returned to his eyes. 'About it not being a pleasure to meet me.'

Love on the Rocks

He chose that moment to lift his glass to his lips, smothering the sly smile that had gave away his amusement at his cheeky line. Kate kept her eyes on his as he sipped, until his glance became more heated than teasing. When she could feel the threat of a blush beginning to spread across her cheeks, she desperately changed tack.

'What d'you do, Roman?' she asked, ignoring her quickened heartbeat.

He swallowed his whiskey. 'I'm a sub-mariner,' he said confidently.

Kate smirked, scooting her drink closer as though she could hide behind it. It took all her composure not to crack a joke about sea-men. 'Yeah, right.'

'I'm stationed at Garden Island,' he continued. His eyes met hers. They were a stormy, intense grey. Suddenly it seemed easier to believe he worked deep beneath the ocean's turbulent surface. 'What do *you* do, Kate?'

'I'm in event management,' she said, hating how superficial it sounded in light of his uber-cool career. She was still almost certain he was lying, and she kicked herself for not having thought of a more interesting line of work to talk about. If she ever did this speed dating thing again, she'd have to say she worked in radio, or that she was a fabulous artist breezing through from Melbourne.

'Interesting,' he mused, lifting his glass again. More whiskey. Wow, this guy was going to wind up with killer stomach ulcers. She tried not to notice the way he licked his lips to savour the taste of the liquor.

Kate raised her brow, having heard the lack of real interest in his tone. 'Really?'

'No, not really. To be honest, I can't think of anything worse than having to run around organising everyone else's party.'

Kate was taken aback by his mean-spirited and rude comment. She wished she hadn't held her off-colour joke. She stared at Roman for a moment, waiting for him to laugh, or tell her that he was only joking. When he did neither, she searched her mind for the perfect comeback.

After a moment, he spoke again. 'You know that the dog thing is the oldest trick in the book, right?'

'What?' Kate snapped. She didn't know whether she was more annoyed he was trying to make fun of Marcus or that he'd so blatantly eavesdropped on their date.

'Mr Puppy-Dog Eyes,' he explained with a cynical smirk. 'The "I love animals" schtick — it's been done to death.'

'So has the "hot asshole" schtick,' Kate snapped. She realised her error immediately.

'You think I'm hot?' He grinned lazily, leaning forward with interest.

Embarrassment and regret flooded her. Giving him the opportunity to pick her apart hadn't been high on her priority list when she'd decided to go through with the evening after their encounter at the bar. Kate narrowed her eyes and crossed her arms over her chest defensively. 'Mostly, I think you're an asshole.'

Love on the Rocks

Roman shrugged. His grin morphed into an arrogant, lopsided smirk. 'In a situation like this, a guy's gotta take what he can get,' he explained.

This guy is unbelievable. Kate quirked a brow. 'And what are you trying to get?' she asked sarcastically.

'A woman who isn't afraid to speak her mind.'

'Ha!' Kate reached for her drink on principle; even though there wasn't any alcohol in it, she'd be happy to have something to spit in his face if he made her laugh again mid-sip.

'What are *you* trying to get?' he asked.

Having a mouth full of juice turned out to be a blessing. Kate held it there for a moment so she could think without blurting out a reply. She swallowed, licking her lips suggestively. With a sassy head-tilt, she threw Roman a slow, triumphant grin.

'A man who isn't interested in speaking at all.'

Although the other couples in the room were all chatting, the silence at their table was deafening. Roman looked shocked, and Kate couldn't tell whether or not he was pleased about it. She held her ground regardless, meeting and holding eye contact. The small plastic alarm clock could be heard now, just above the din, ticking down as time ran out.

It was impossible to tell whether he would accept her challenge. Whatever Roman was thinking, he hid it well. What would he say, and what would she say *back*?

Perhaps she had stepped over the line. But at the end of the day, wasn't the whole point about this speed dating malarkey to explore uncharted territory? She'd come out tonight to push her own boundaries. In part, Kate had hoped to find out how strong the bond really was between Greg and herself. She supposed the situation had reached critical mass.

His intense grey eyes were unreadable, but Kate braved the storm. His gaze burned across her face, falling to her lips before travelling lower. Was he checking her out, or conceding defeat?

Another few seconds revealed it was possibly a bit of both. Roman stood, shrugging his jacket into place over his broad shoulders. Kate watched wordlessly as he prepared to leave, unsure whether to be pleased she had beaten him at his own game, or be disappointed he wasn't as resilient as he had made out.

When he held his hand out to her, she didn't hesitate to accept it. They left the small, cosy bar together, the alarm clock thwarted in its countdown.

Kate was glad she'd sprung for a taxi instead of driving herself. It would have been a shame to miss riding in his sleek, black BMW. She trotted across the car park towards it, not wanting to give him the opportunity to open the door for her. The leather seats were cool to the touch as she slid into the car. A moment later, he joined her.

'You look like you're in shock,' she said smugly.

'I wasn't expecting you to say that, back there,' he admitted, reaching to buckle up. His aftershave filled the car, enveloping her. Kate instantly felt her stomach flop, the way it did when she rode elevators. It was light, spicy, and somehow made her feel like she was drunk even though all she'd had that evening was orange juice on the rocks.

'Get used to it,' she told him, leaning back against the seat, 'if you really want a woman who speaks her mind.'

Second later, they were on their way back to her place. The car's powerful engine lulled her; she'd always loved fast cars. Her fingers caressed the buttery leather of the seat as she watched the dark streets zip past. When she turned her head to look at Roman, she noticed him glancing at her hand, his expression serious. Was he just going to drop her off?

'What else is on your mind?' he asked instead.

His hands gripped the fancy steering wheel, almost like he was restraining himself. Kate smiled slyly, angling herself to face him. 'Wouldn't you like to know?' she teased, adding, 'turn right here.'

The car veered right. Roman threaded the wheel through his hands, a manoeuvre she was sure he hadn't learned as a *sub-mariner*. 'That's why I asked,' he said, flicking her a sidelong glance.

'Next left.'

While he concentrated on the road, she took the chance to thoroughly examine his looks. He had a Roman nose, sure enough, presiding over full lips that looked just as sexy when they were serious as they did when he was smirking at her. She let them monopolise her view. 'I'm wondering what else you would be looking for in a woman,' she admitted. Her voice was low and seductive, in a way that surprised her.

It didn't seem to surprise him. Roman laughed; the kind of breathy laugh of someone more flattered than amused. 'And?' he prompted.

Kate sat up straighter, folding her hands into her lap. 'I think you don't really know what you want.'

They paused at a set of traffic lights on Read Street. As soon as the car purred to a halt, Roman turned to her. Suddenly his face was much, much closer. Kate's eyes widened as he glanced at her lips. Acting on instinct, she leaned closer. His breath was tantalisingly warm across her cheek, and she took a deeper breath so she could drink him in. If she tilted her head just right, their lips would touch.

'What makes you say that?' he murmured, looking back into her eyes.

'You say you want a woman who speaks her mind,' Kate said softly, 'but the instant I did — at the bar — you were rude about it.' She worried that she would blink and break the spell he had cast on her. He smelled amazing, and she felt her attraction to him take a flying leap as he offered her a slow, knowing smile.

'Maybe I was trying to draw you out of your shell,' he whispered, inching closer.

Kate's heart skipped a beat. Her lips parted slightly, and she closed her eyes in anticipation of the kiss that was about to rock her world.

They both jumped when an angry car horn reminded them the traffic lights had turned green.

Love on the Rocks

Kate reached backwards, fumbling to get her keys into the door with one hand. Her other hand grasped the collar of Roman's shirt, pulling him forward. Their frantic kiss broke momentarily until Roman stepped closer. He chased her, dipping his head so their lips remained close but not meeting as they tumbled through the suddenly open door. Kate carelessly shoved it closed with her foot.

He scooped her closer with one arm. The leather of his jacket felt hot to the touch, and Kate lost herself in the sensation before realising it was nothing compared to the scorching heat of his kisses as he explored her neck. She leaned into him, revelling in the way his body fit snugly against hers. The fresh night air lingered in the hallway, the nights still cold enough to make her glad of the extra body heat. It was close, sexy. *Intimate*.

'I think you want what every man wants,' she continued, closing her eyes lightly as he paused just beneath her ear.

'Maybe I do, right this minute,' he smiled, his breath caressing the gentle curve of her shoulder.

Kate was taken in for a moment, her fingertips resting lightly against the promise of finely crafted muscles beneath the polo he was wearing. But she didn't want to be misunderstood, and if this was going to be a one-off thing then she needed to make sure her point got across. She pulled back slightly to look into his face.

'I mean, I think you want a dutiful Stepford wife, who waits on you hand and foot.'

Roman grinned, cheeky confidence plain on his face. 'That'd be nice,' he teased, looking past Kate at the table in the hallway. He nodded at a cluster of photo frames, next to a little wooden sign that said 'family'. 'Is that what your husband wanted?'

'He never knew *what* he wanted,' Kate admitted, shaking her head. 'Still doesn't.'

It wasn't hard to push aside memories of Greg in that moment. The way Roman looked down at her seemed like a silent appeal, as though he was begging her to prove that she knew what *she* wanted, regardless. Kate began to undo the buttons on Roman's polo, intent on providing herself with a distraction. He had a decent tan that made her think he spent a good deal of time outdoors. A light dusting of chest hair was visible, before Roman leaned in close to her. She glanced down at his chest, before meeting his gaze.

'What else do you think I want?' he smirked.

'A woman who earns her own money, so she's not spending yours,' Kate murmured, a wry smile working its way onto her kiss-ripened lips. Her fingers made a grab for his shirt, which she used to pull him closer. They overbalanced slightly, and Roman used the momentum to press her against the wall.

'It's important to be independent.' He kept his lips close to hers as he spoke, slyly inviting her to close the gap. 'Even if you're faffing about, running parties.'

There was nothing more appealing to her than verbal foreplay. Roman had been her best option for the night ever since the two formidable syllables he had offered her at the bar. Somewhere between the car and the door, Kate had lost her cardigan. She shivered, but not because she felt cold.

'And I think that you're—'

She forgot what she was saying as he caressed her. He skirted the neckline of her top, slowly and deliberately drawing a line across her chest that made her skin tingle. Her breath caught in her throat and she arched her back towards him, silently pushing away from the wall as she waited for more. Roman obliged. His feathery stroke evolved until his hand massaged her breast, and Kate allowed herself a breathy gasp as his touch echoed through her body.

'You're—' she gasped, as he pulled down the neckline of her top, expertly pushing aside the cup of her bra. Her second attempt to finish her sentence was cut short, when he crushed his lips to hers. His tongue was soft but insistent, and Kate found herself fighting against the instinctive haze that threatened to overtake her. Her left nipple throbbed as he rolled it between his fingertips, making the other one desperate for attention. Kate cleared her throat inelegantly, her breath coming faster.

As he bent to kiss her through the thin, stretchy fabric of her top, Kate finally found her voice.

'You're going to have to do better than *that*,' she warned, huskily. He grinned against her breast, and she took the moment of respite to reach for his hand. She led him through the house in search of the bedroom. Her body ached at the absence of him; she didn't know what she would do after, but for now none of that mattered.

They made it into the kitchen before he held her back, turning her away from her single-minded mission. He shoved one of the kitchen table chairs to one side with his other hand. The next moment he stepped toward her, his foot between hers. Kate stepped back, until she felt the hard edge of the table meet her bum.

'You're the kind of woman who likes a challenge,' Roman said, reaching to cup her cheek. It was an action that could have been tender, even sweet. She had seen it a hundred times in movies, smooth and platonic. This was nothing like that, she realised, as his rigid length pressed suggestively against the front of her skirt.

'Maybe,' she said, holding her breath as she looked him in the eye.

'– and who isn't afraid to be honest,' he continued. He stooped slightly for a moment, breathing hard at the friction as his other hand reached down to grip the hem of her skirt. Kate's own breath was ragged, but escalated to a gasp as he wrenched the denim up. She felt fit to burst out of her skin.

'If you want my opinion,' she agreed, moving to pop the button of his jeans, 'you'd better be ready for it.'

'Really?' He paused, watching as she tugged his zipper. Before long he stood in front of her, straining against his boxers. Kate wriggled backwards, sitting up onto the table and hooking her foot around Roman's leg to bring him in to meet her. Finally, there was nothing more than a flimsy cotton barrier between them.

'What do you think?' he asked her hoarsely.

'I think it's time that we shut up,' she smiled, gripping his shirt to pull him towards her as she leaned back on the table.

Bacon sizzled in the frying pan, lulling a tired Kate into a state of waking unconsciousness. Ever since she woke to find herself in an empty bed, sheets rumpled and smelling like Roman, she'd been smothered with memories of the night before. A slow, lazy smile hovered on her lips as she flipped her egg, and enjoyed the peaceful solitude of her Sunday morning.

The sound of the garage door going up and Greg's car pulling in forced her back to reality. Butterflies instantly flooded her stomach, and she turned to face the frying pan. When Greg came in, he would get a brilliant view of the back of Kate's head.

The door opened. 'Morning,' Greg said tentatively. Over the hiss of the bacon, she heard him rest his overnight bag on the kitchen table. Kate only just managed to stop herself from indulging in another fanciful flashback.

Greg hovered by the breakfast bar. 'That smells amazing.'

'Mmm,' Kate managed.

'What time do you have to collect Jenna?'

Good. Talking about Jenna would give her enough time to decide what she'd say about last night. 'Not until after lunch.'

There was a short silence. A moment later, Kate felt Greg move to stand close behind her. His touch was different to those she experienced the night before. Where Roman had been daring and insistent, Greg was gentle and familiar. For the first time in a long time, Kate let herself relax against him. Her head rested on his shoulder, as he cuddled her.

'Time for round two?' he asked, coyly.

Kate craned her neck, leaning back slightly so that she could look at him. His hair was in its usual style, combed neatly back from his face in a way that accentuated his playful gaze. The trendy hairstyle that Roman had worn was gone without a trace, but something in the way he smirked at her reminded Kate that maybe — just *maybe* — Roman might make future appearances in their bedroom roster.

'That depends,' Kate grinned, turning the bacon.

'On?' Greg slipped a soft kiss onto her neck.

'On how many other speed dates you picked up last night.'

There was laughter in his voice when he answered her. 'Babe.' He pulled her closer, his arms wrapping around her waist. 'You'll always be more than enough woman for me.'

Warmth spread through Kate. She smiled as she realised that the man she had been looking for had been there all along. Even with his stuffy ways, and his unfashionable hair, Greg still knew how to make her feel exceptional. She basked in the nearness of him, taking in the scent of his normal aftershave, when she remembered something.

'I've never seen you drink straight liquor like that,' she teased, glancing over her shoulder at him. 'What whiskey was it, anyway? I might get a bottle, for special occasions.'

'It wasn't whiskey,' Greg grinned. 'It was iced tea.'

Louisa Loder

Thank you for reading *Love on the rocks*.
We hope you enjoyed it.

If you enjoyed it, please consider leaving an honest review on Goodreads or Amazon. Reviews can help readers find books and we would be grateful for your help. Thank you for taking the time to let others know what you thought.

If you'd like to know more about Louisa, or connect with her online, please visit her webpage louisaloder.com, follow her on Twitter @louisaloder, or like her Facebook page https://www.facebook.com/louisaloderauthor/

This book was published by Serenity Press under its Serenity Romance imprint. If you'd like to see what else Serenity Press publishes, visit serenitypress.org

Louisa Loder

Louisa likes Pina Coladas and gettin' caught in the rain. Determined to empty her brain of stories, she writes across several genres including fantasy, speculative fiction, and romance. Her fantasy novella *Stormfate* was released earlier in 2015, and she is an avid writer of short stories – some of which are available for free on her website.

She lives in Mandurah, Western Australia, and drinks more coffee than is good for her. When she's not writing or researching projects, Louisa enjoys spending time with her family. Hobbies include playing video games, watching copious amounts of tv, and various craft-related initiatives.

She strongly believes that the truth is still out there. Her website is www.louisaloder.com

www.ingramcontent.com/pod-product-compliance
Lightning Source LLC
Chambersburg PA
CBHW021137300426
44113CB00006B/463